Miranda Peabody and the Magnificent Friendship March

A Story About Bullies, Bystanders and Friendship

By: Susan DeBell, PhD

youth light
inc.

© 2008 by
YouthLight, Inc.
Chapin, SC 29036

All rights reserved.
Permission is given for individual educators and counselors to reproduce activities indicated for use.
Reproduction of these materials for an entire school system is strictly prohibited.

Project Layout by Amy Rule
Project Editing by Susan Bowman

ISBN 1-59850-053-8
EAN 978-1-59850-053-0

Library of Congress
2007943886

10 9 8 7 6 5 4 3 2 1
Printed in the United States of America

Dedication

To anyone who is being bullied or has been bullied. May you find strength, support, and hope from your friends. May you find courage, conviction, and endurance within yourself.

It was a bright, sunny day at Mountain Stream Elementary
School. Miranda Peabody and her friends were looking forward
to an exciting new school year.

© YouthLight, Inc.

After lunch, Miranda and her friends Patricia Greenwood, Arlene Lee, and Thomas Kulpowski were playing marbles on the blacktop near the kindergarten door.

© YouthLight, Inc.

Suddenly, a loud, mean, and scary voice rang out from behind the large evergreen tree... "Hey, clear the way; I'm mean Maxie Baxter and this is my playground!"

© YouthLight, Inc.

When Miranda and her friends looked up, they saw a girl about their height with a very angry-looking face stomping towards them.

© YouthLight, Inc.

Two other students Donald Driverson and Patsy Griffer stood nearby and looked angry as well.

"This is my playground," Maxie shouted, "You and your friends better leave or you'll be sorry!"

"No way," Miranda replied, "this is our playground and we are staying!"

Miranda's friends were frightened and told Miranda that they'd better leave.

© YouthLight, Inc.

Running away, they left their marbles and their lunchboxes.

"I'll get you good!" warned Maxie as Miranda and her friends ran back towards the building.

© YouthLight, Inc.

Miranda and her friends spent the rest of their recess time wondering how a person could be so angry and trying to decide what to do next. They decided the best thing to do was to tell their parents about Maxie and what was happening to them.

They didn't tell their teacher Ms. Klemp, because they were afraid that Maxie and the other students would make things even worse if they found out that Miranda and her friends had told their teacher about what was going on.

© YouthLight, Inc.

When Miranda told her parents, they gave her a big hug and told her to ignore Maxie's mean words.

Patricia Greenwood's mom told her to do something kind for Maxie, because she had low self-esteem and that made her want to be a bully.

© YouthLight, Inc.

9

Thomas Kulpowski's grandmother gave him boxing lessons so he could defend himself against bullies.

© YouthLight, Inc.

The next day Miranda followed her parents' advice and tried ignoring Maxie's unkind words and angry threats,

but this only made Maxie more determined, and she continued teasing Miranda and the others.

© YouthLight, Inc.

Thomas Kulpowski put on his grandmother's boxing gloves to defend himself, but Maxie only laughed at him and pushed him out of the way. Thomas fell down and scraped both of his knees. The crowd of students watching all of this began laughing and cheering Maxie on!

© YouthLight, Inc.

Patricia Greenwood brought Maxie a special cupcake with pink sprinkles,

but Maxie laughed and stomped it into the ground with her large green work boots. This made Patricia cry.

TO MAXIE

© YouthLight, Inc.

© YouthLight, Inc.

Other student's in Miranda's class wanted to help their friends, but they were too frightened to do anything and just stood by.

They were afraid that if they spoke out, they too would become victims of Maxie's bullying.

© YouthLight, Inc.

Finally, Miranda and her friends knew they had to stop Maxie and her followers,

so they told their teacher
Ms. Klemp what had been going
on at recess. "Ms. Klemp," they cried,
"Maxie Baxter is teasing and bothering us
and nothing we've tried to do has stopped her!"

16

© YouthLight, Inc.

"I must tell Principal Appleberry!," exclaimed Ms. Klemp. "We can't have this bullying and teasing going on here in Mountain Stream School.

We must start an anti-bullying campaign right away! Meanwhile, you and your friends have to get the rest of the students on your side," explained Ms Klemp. "Talk to the bystanders – the boys and girls who have been watching all of this and encouraging Maxie and the ones who are too frightened to tell anyone – and get them to help."

© YouthLight, Inc.

"I know," exclaimed Miranda,
"Let's have a No More Bullies Campaign!

We can make signs and hang them up in the hallways. We can ask other teachers to have class meetings and talk about bullying and how important it is to report bullying when it happens so that bullies like Maxie can be stopped."

© YouthLight, Inc.

"I'll ask Mrs. Lee our music teacher to have a special program for all of the students and teachers about friendship and the importance of respecting everyone and being kind to every student in our school.

Even bullies like Maxie," said Ms. Klemp.

© YouthLight, Inc.

Everyone, including
Ms. Klemp, Mrs. Lee, and Principal
Appleberry agreed that all of these
ideas should be started right away, so the next day
Miranda and her friends made many anti-bullying signs and
with Principal Appleberry's permission, began hanging them
up all over the school. Miranda, her friends, and even some
of the students who had been too frightened to confront
the bully decided to have a peace and friendship march
during recess the following afternoon.

© YouthLight, Inc.

Principal Appleberry then spoke to Maxie in his office and told her that her bullying must stop. There would be no more bullying allowed at school!

© YouthLight, Inc.

Then Principal Appleberry had a special teacher's meeting and explained the new anti-bullying program called "Up With Friends – Down With Bullies!" He told them that the program was to take place immediately and even announced it in the parent newsletter that went home that week.

© YouthLight, Inc.

When the other students found out about the "Up With Friends – Down With Bullies Program" they made signs too. Even Patsy, Donald, and the students that had encouraged Maxie to be mean joined in. Many students, teachers, and parents worked together to make the school a more peaceful place.

© YouthLight, Inc.

"If we all stick together, bullies like Maxie can't frighten and hurt us!" exclaimed Miranda.

Principal Appleberry and Ms. Klemp agreed.

© YouthLight, Inc.

The next day with Miranda in the lead, twenty-six students walked out onto the blacktop near the kindergarten door.

Carrying some of their signs, they shouted, "No more bullies! Down with bullies...up with friends!"

© YouthLight, Inc.

Maxie soon came stomping down the path, ready to frighten Miranda and her friends and expecting the other students to join in.

© YouthLight, Inc.

"Maxie, no more bullies are allowed here at school," stated Miranda using a calm, firm voice, looking right into Maxie's angry face. Miranda stood straight and tall so that Maxie would know that she wasn't afraid and meant every word she said. "No more bullies!" shouted the others as they walked towards Maxie.

© YouthLight, Inc.

Maxie was very amazed at what was happening, and to everyone's surprise, she stepped back and started to cry!

"I was mean, because I wanted everyone to respect me," she sobbed. "In my other school, people made fun of me, so I thought that if I became a bully, I could be in charge and could feel important."

© YouthLight, Inc.

"Maxie," said Miranda softly, "if you want to be part of the school and have others respect you, you have to be kind. If you're mean and make others feel bad, everyone will be afraid of you and no one will ever be your friend."

"I'm sorry," sobbed Maxie, "I would like to be friends with everyone!"

© YouthLight, Inc.

Miranda slowly reached into her pocket and pulled out a beautiful, clear blue marble. She then gave it to Maxie. It was Miranda's favorite and the only marble that had not been left behind on the day that Maxie began her bullying.

"This is for you, Maxie," said Miranda, "apology accepted!" As Maxie took the marble, the other students cheered loudly and waved their signs.

© YouthLight, Inc.

Then to everyone's surprise, Maxie took a large sign and with a black crayon added, "I, Maxie Baxter, declare, NO MORE BULLIES!"

© YouthLight, Inc.

Everyone continued cheering and began singing the school song while Ms. Klemp, Mrs. Lee, and Principal Appleberry watched from the classroom windows.

© YouthLight, Inc.

A very broad smile was seen across all of their faces as they all were certain that Mountain Stream Elementary School had become a place of friendship and respect.

© YouthLight, Inc.

Discussion Questions

1. What is a bully and why do people become bullies?

2. How did the students react to Maxie and what did they do to try to stop the bullying?

3. Think of a time when you were bullied. What did you do to stop it?

4. What did Ms. Klemp tell Miranda and her friends to do to stop the bullying at Mountain Steam Elementary School?

5. What is a bystander and how do bystanders contribute to bullying?

6. How did Mountain Stream Elementary School finally become a place of peace, friendship, and respect?

Answers

1. A bully is someone who gets power by being mean and scaring others so that he or she can be in charge.

2. The students were scared of Maxie and ran away. They tried to stop the bullying by telling their parents, but the things their parents told them to do did not stop Maxie from bullying them.

3. Student answers individually.

4. Ms. Klemp told Miranda and her friends to get the other students – the bystanders to help end the bullying.

5. A bystander is someone who watches silently while someone else gets bullied. Often he or she would like to help, but being afraid and not knowing what to do often stops bystanders from helping the victim. Standing by and doing nothing tells the bully that it is all right to be mean to other people. Some bystanders even encourage bullying by joining in and telling the bully to keep being mean.

6. When Miranda and her friends decided to have a "No More Bullies Campaign" the other children joined in and helped Maxie to realize that it is better to be a friend than a bully. This made their school a more peaceful and loving place.

"No More Bullies" Activity

Name _____   Date _____

Pretend you are part of Miranda's "No More Bullies Campaign."

Draw yourself and a sign that tells others how you feel about bullies.

Miranda's Marble Activity

Name _____   Date _____

Color Miranda's marbles. Then label each one with ways of stopping a bully.

(For example, speaking firmly to a bully, walking and standing straight and tall, making eye contact, telling an adult, getting friends to help, etc.)

Bully / Victim Portrait Activity

Name _____   Date _____

Do you know what a bully and a victim might look like?
Draw a picture of each and then tell a partner how each
one behaves and how to avoid becoming a victim or a bully.

Please Help the Bystanders Activity

Name _____   Date _____

Write some ways to stop a bully on the "What to Do List"
so that these bystanders will know how to help a victim.

Remember: If you just stand by and watch bullying
happen or join in the teasing, you are telling the
bully it's OK to hurt someone else!!

What to do ^about bullies List...

1. _____

_____

2. _____

_____

3. _____

_____

4. _____

_____

MARBLES